You Renewed

21 Day Experience

Take a Chance on Yourself for Just 21 Days.
You Will Be So Glad You Did.
You Will Be Renewed!

Coach K.

M000115220

ISBN 978-1-0980-7614-6 (paperback)
ISBN 978-1-0980-7615-3 (digital)

Copyright © 2021 by Coach K.

All rights reserved. No part of this publication may be reproduced, distributed, or transmitted in any form or by any means, including photocopying, recording, or other electronic or mechanical methods without the prior written permission of the publisher. For permission requests, solicit the publisher via the address below.

Christian Faith Publishing, Inc.
832 Park Avenue
Meadville, PA 16335
www.christianfaithpublishing.com

Printed in the United States of America

Contents

You Renewed Experience Introduction

Hello, You Renewed team members! First of all, thank you so very much for participating in this 21-day You Renewed experience. I promise you will be glad you did. Second and most important, congratulations for taking the steps toward You Renewed.

I know you all are very busy. Some of you have started school, have children starting school, and have new jobs and new homes, and some of you are just busy. Being busy is a fantastic thing, because no matter what your schedule or where you are in your life, this experience will fit right in.

So, since we are all so busy, let's get right to it.

The You Renewed Experience

Have you heard Albert Einstein's quote "If you fail to plan, you plan to fail"? Well, failure is not an option; therefore, the *You Renewed 21-Day Experience* plan is as follows:

You can start the experience anytime you wish; however, I recommend starting on a Sunday for easier tracking.

For even better results, please visit the following social media pages:

- twitter.com/URenewedFitness
- Instagram @yourenewedexperience

The program has five equally important segments:

- Spiritual
- Goal
- Motivational
- Physical
- Emotional

Spiritual—"In everything you do, put God first, and He will direct you and crown your efforts with success" (Proverbs 3:6).

I am a strong believer that when you put God first in all that you do, the only possible outcome is what *His* will is for you. Therefore, each day will start with a scripture to kick off your experience. You will be amazed at how the scripture will be very relevant to your respective goal.

Goal—"He who fails to plan is planning to fail" (Winston Churchill).

With every great plan, there is some kind of achievement or goal to accomplish. The *You Renewed 21-Day Experience* is a great plan, so you will establish a goal.

Over the next couple of days, think about what a You Renewed looks like. It takes 21 days to form a habit, so what do you want to accomplish in 21 days, and what are you working toward? Well, you are probably asking, What is this "experience" that can I accomplish? I'm glad you asked.

The next great thing about this experience is that your goal, your achievement, is completely up to you. If you want to eat better, this experience is for you. If you want to become more active, this experience is for you. If you feel you need a bit more discipline in your life, this experience is for you. If you want to lose a few pounds, this experience is for you. Is there something happening in your life you feel is out of your control and you just want a breakthrough? This experience is for you.

How is that, you ask? The *You Renewed 21-Day Experience* is about motivating you spiritually, emotionally, physically, and mentally.

With all that said, over the next couple of days, really think about a specific, measurable, attainable, relevant goal, and you will see results with the You Renewed experience in 21 days.

Every day, you will be asked to write and say your goal out loud. Below are three examples of You Renewed goals:

Example 1

Goal:
Say this out loud: *I will see success with (write you goal here)* <u>reading and retaining 1 scripture a day for 21 days and then it becoming a habit after the 21 days</u>

_____

on the other side of my You Renewed 21-Day Experience!

Example 2

Goal:
Say this out loud: *I will see success with (write you goal here)* <u>drinking 16–32 ounces of water every day when I wake up, when I am hungry, before and after every meal, and before and after any workout</u>

_____

on the other side of my You Renewed 21-Day Experience!

Example 3

Goal:
Say this out loud: *I will see success with (write your goal here)* <u>understanding what I have to change in my life to fix my relationship with my best friend of 20 years</u>

_____

on the other side of my You Renewed 21-Day Experience!

If you have a weight-loss goal or a goal to simply become more active, I highly recommend a before and after picture. The picture can be a real-life picture or a picture with your specific measurements. If you choose the picture with the measurements, you will need a body tape measure. Be sure to capture your results on the results/change-it-up days.

Another great tool to use if you have a weight-loss goal is a body-fat calculator. I have found that this measurement is a far better measurement to track results.

- Log the measurements into the following calculator: http://www.calculator.net/body-fat-calculator.html.
- An indication of what to strive for, over time, for men is 8–15% and for women is 13.5–22%.

Motivational—"Believe in yourself and all that you are. Know that there is something inside you that is greater than any obstacle" (Christian D. Larson).

Everyone does better when they feel better, and one of the best ways to feel better is with motivation and encouragement; therefore, each day, you are provided with a motivational quote to encourage you for the day.

Physical—"I never could have achieved the success that I have without physical activity and health goals" (Bonnie Blair).

In my journey, this part of the experience has always been the most challenging because it has the most impact on your physical appearance. However, because it is extremely important, I worked very hard to ensure it is as simple as possible.

When you look good, you feel good! Even though you *all* already look good, this very simple daily dose of physical activity will take you to another level.

There are four parts to the physical:

1. *Exercise*
A. Morning plank—Each morning, you will be provided 1-minute plank exercise.

Benefits of the planking:

1. Planking helps to build your deep inner core muscles and also helps to lay the groundwork toward developing the six-pack look.
2. Over time, the muscles around your shoulders, collar-bone, shoulder blades, hamstrings, and even the arches in your feet will stretch, which will in turn increase flexibility.
3. As you increase your strength and flexibility, you will also increase your stability and improve your balance.
4. One of the best side effects of plank exercises is reducing back pain. Due to the core strengthening received from planks, your lower back is strengthened as well.
   - Beginners—Always start on your elbows and knees.

   Elbow plank (knee)
   - Intermediate—Start in the beginner position, lift your legs, tighten your gluteus, and straighten your back.

   Elbow plank
   - Advanced—Start in the intermediate position, and straighten your arms. Remember to tighten your glutes and straighten your back.

B. Strength exercises—Each day, you will have a set of three 1-minute strength exercises to complete. Don't worry, there will be 6 days of rest throughout the 21-day experience. There will also be a link to the "Your Renewed" experience YouTube to demonstrate the exercises.

Benefits of the strength training:

1. It is *fantastic* for your heart health.
2. It is an *awesome* stress reliever.
3. Over time, you will burn more calories while you rest.
4. You will build stronger bones.
5. You will lose fat and look slimmer.

C. Thirty-minute walk—Each day, you will be encouraged to walk at least 30 minutes. If you find you don't have time to walk for 30 minutes, break it up into three 10-minute walks or ensure you get 10,000 steps in a day. Over time, you should be able to walk 2 miles in 30 minutes.

Benefits of walking:

1. Maintain a healthy weight.
2. Improve your mood.
3. Improve your coordination and balance.

Note: Exercise tips to keep in mind

• Purchase a pedometer to track your steps.
• *Do not* overextend yourself. You will counter the effects of the physical portion of your experience. Therefore, during all physical activity, ensure you are able to sing a song or carry a conversation. If you cannot, *stop rest for 30 seconds to a minute* and then continue.
• The strength exercises can be accomplished as active rest intervals during the 30-minute walk.
• As you progress, you can add weights.

2. *Meals*

   I love to eat, so I ensured the program included food, food, and more food. It is very important to eat 3 meals a day. Each meal should be broken up into 4 parts. The 4 parts can be any combination of fruit and/or vegetable, fat, and meat. For example, you can have 2 meats, a vegetable, and a fat; 2 fats, a meat, and a fruit/vegetable; or 2 fruits/vegetables, a fat, and a meat. It doesn't matter the combination as long as you eat the meal, and it is only composed of those four parts. Don't worry, I will provide you with examples as well as seasoning techniques that will be both tasteful and results oriented.

3. *Snacking*

   Each day, I encourage you to have 3–4 snacks. Hmm, snacks! I will provide you with a list of tasteful and results-oriented snacks. Also, as a reward to all of the hard work you will be accomplishing throughout your experience, you will have "treat" days.

4. *Drinking*

   This part of the experience is probably the absolute most important. *Do not skip, change, or divert from this part in any way.* Drink 16–32 ounces of *cool / not cold* water as soon as you get up in the mornings, before and after each meal, and before and after your exercise. If you are a coffee drinker, limit your coffee intake to 1–2 cups a day with no more than 2 tbs. of sugar-free sweetener. If you drink alcohol, no mixed drinks, only 1 glass of wine or 1 beer, and this will count as one of your snacks ;-). Please do not drink any sugary drinks like sweet tea, carbonated drinks, sports drinks, or energy drinks during this 21-day You Renewed experience. Lastly, before bed, enjoy a cup of herbal tea with lemon and/or ginger.

Emotional—"Our emotions need to be as educated as our intellect. It is important to know how to feel, how to respond and how to let life in so that it can touch you" (Anonymous).

It is proven that writing removes mental blocks, so the final part of the *You Renewed 21-Day Experience* is journaling. During the experience, you will be encouraged to journal your experience starting with writing down your specific, measurable, attainable, relevant goal and ending with whatever is on your mind about the day.

Alrighty then, that is the *You Renewed 21-Day Experience*. If you still want to participate, and I truly hope you do, simply start!

A little bit more, some tools you will need throughout your experience:

- A body tape measure.
- Some kind of stopwatch to time your exercises. Don't worry, you will not do anything other than the walk for longer than 1 minute.
- Of course, something to journal in that is dedicated to this experience and, lastly, an open mind.

The last thing I ask, please share this program with any and everyone you know. The point of the program is exactly what the title says to renew you, and we are all a work in progress and need to take a few days every so often and renew.

Thank you again, and I look forward to seeing ***You Renewed*** on the other side of your 21-day experience.

Love you all!

Coach K

PS: Read through this multiple times and send me as many questions and any feedback as possible to YouRenewedExperience@gmail.com.

On your mark…get set…*get renewed*!

Wait. Before we get going, I want to share with you some of the concerns I know you have:

- *I am not sure I can commit to 21 days*—We have *all* wasted 21 days in our lives some time or another. I *promise* you, committing to this 21-day experience is not going to be easy in the beginning, but you *will* see results and you *will* want to see what is going to happen on the other side of the 21 days. I *promise*. In the beginning, you are likely to stop. That is okay. You have all 21 days at your fingertips. I encourage you to complete the entire 21 days, but you can break it up however you feel would give you the success you are looking for.
- *I don't have the time needed to do this*—I am a single mother of a very active young son, I have a demanding job, I participate in 3 ministries with my church, I offer private training, I work out 4–5 times a week, and other stuff. I didn't share that to recommend doing a whole lot of stuff. I shared it to let you know you have time. I have made it as simple as possible to incorporate this program into any day. I *strongly* recommend committing to a renewed you and I *promise* you have time for that. If you still feel you do not, keeping it 100, this program isn't for you, and *you simply just don't want to participate*, and that is *totally* okay. Every decision we make has a consequence. It's up to you on whether that consequence is a negative or a positive one. Participating in this experience will translate to nothing but positive consequences. I *promise*!

Now, let's get **You Renewed**.

Your 21-Day
You Renewed Experience

Hello, You Renewed team members! Congratulations on starting the You Renewed 21-Day Program! Below is day 1.

Scripture:
Jeremiah 29:11 (MSG)—"I know what I'm doing. I have it all planned out—plans to take care of you, not to abandon you, plans to give you the future you hope for."

Goal:
<u>Say this out loud:</u> *I will see success (write your goal here)*
_____
_____
_____
_____
_____
_____

on the other side of my You Renewed 21-Day Experience!

Motivation:
"You don't have to be great to get started, you just have to get started to be GREAT!" (Cathy Carpenter).

Physical:
- *Water—Drink 16–32 ounces at the following intervals:*
  - As soon as you wake up
  - Before and after your meals
  - Before and after your workouts
- Meals—3 per day (meal prep is an excellent way to ensure success)
  - Weight loss option—35% protein, 40% fruits and vegetables, and 25% fat
  - Toning option—40% protein, 35% fruits and vegetables, and 25% fats
- *Snacks—Refer to the approved optimal results list.*
  - Eat at least 4–5 snacks 1–2 hours before and/or after each meal.

- Workout—We start with our arms.
  - Wake-up plank—1 minute (please remember to stop your timer when you rest)
    - Regular plank
  - Strength exercises—1 minute each (please do 3–4 rounds)
    - 1-minute push-ups
    - 1-minute plank—Again? Yes!
    - 1-minute arm circles
  - 30-minute walk

Emotional:
Please do not forget to journal your experience.

_____

_____

_____

I love you all, and I will see you on the other side of the 21-day experience.

Coach K
#armsday #ismile

YOU RENEWED

_____
_____
_____
_____
_____
_____
_____
_____
_____
_____
_____
_____
_____
_____
_____
_____
_____
_____
_____
_____
_____

Hello, You Renewed team members! Congratulations on making it through day 1 and to day 2. Below is day 2.

Scripture:
Isaiah 40:31—"But they who wait for the LORD shall renew their strength; they shall mount up with wings like eagles; they shall run and not be weary; they shall walk and not faint."

Goal:
Say this out loud: *I will see success (write your goal here)*

_____

_____

_____

_____

_____

on the other side of my You Renewed 21-Day Experience!

Motivation:
"You live longer once you realize that any time spent being unhappy is wasted" (Ruth E. Renkel).

Physical:
- *Water—Drink 16–32 ounces at the following intervals:*
  - As soon as you wake up
  - Before and after your meals
  - Before and after your workouts
- Meals—3 per day (meal prep is an excellent way to ensure success)
  - Weight loss option—35% protein, 40% fruits and vegetables, and 25% fat
  - Toning option—40% protein, 35% fruits and vegetables, and 25% fats
- *Snacks—Refer to the approved optimal results list.*
  - Eat at least 4–5 snacks 1–2 hours before and/or after each meal.

- Workout—We start with our arms.
  - Wake-up plank—1 minute (please remember to stop your timer when you rest)
    - Leg out plank—While in the plank position, alternate stepping each leg to the side and back in.
  - Strength exercises—1 minute each (please do 3–4 rounds)
    - Yoga—warrior one
    - Yoga—warrior two
    - Yoga—warrior three
  - 30-minute walk

Emotional:
Please do not forget to journal your experience.

_____
_____
_____

I love you all, and I will see you on the other side of the 21-day experience.

Coach K
#legsday #ismile

Hello, You Renewed team members! Congratulations on making it through day 2 and to day 3. Below is day 3.

Scripture:
Isaiah 41:10—"So do not fear, for I am with you; do not be dismayed, for I am your God. I will strengthen you and help you; I will uphold you with my righteous right hand."

Goal:
Say this out loud: *I will see success (write your goal here)*

_____

_____

_____

_____

_____

on the other side of my You Renewed 21-Day Experience!

Motivation:
"Today is my tomorrow. It's up to me to shape it, to take control and seize every opportunity. The power is in the choices I make each day. I eat well, I live well. I shape me!" (Motivationblog.org).

Physical:
- *Water—Drink 16–32 ounces at the following intervals:*
  - As soon as you wake up
  - Before and after your meals
  - Before and after your workouts
- Meals—3 per day (meal prep is an excellent way to ensure success)
  - Weight loss option—35% protein, 40% fruits and vegetables, and 25% fat
  - Toning option—40% protein, 35% fruits and vegetables, and 25% fats

- *Snacks—Refer to the approved optimal results list.*
  - Eat at least 4–5 snacks 1–2 hours before and/or after each meal.
- Workout—We start with our arms.
  - Wake-up plank—1 minute (please remember to stop your timer when you rest)
  - Up down plank—While in the plank position, alternate going from your forearms to your hands.
  - Strength exercises—1 minute each (please do 3–4 rounds)
    - V-ups
    - Brazilian sit-ups
    - Lying overhead reach
  - 30-minute walk

Emotional:
Please do not forget to journal your experience.

_____
_____

_____

I love you all, and I will see you on the other side of the 21-day experience.

Coach K
#absday #ismile

YOU RENEWED

Hello, You Renewed team members! Congratulations on making it through day 3 and to day 4. Below is day 4.

Scripture:
John 14:27 (AMP)—"Peace I leave with you; my own peace I now give and bequeath to you. Not as the world gives do I give to you. Do not let your hearts be troubled, neither let them be afraid. [Stop allowing yourselves to be agitated and disturbed; and do not permit yourselves to be fearful and intimidated and cowardly and unsettled.]"

Goal:
Say this out loud: *I will see success (write your goal here)*
_____
_____
_____
_____
_____
_____

on the other side of my You Renewed 21-Day Experience!

Motivation:
"When you feel like quitting, think about why you started" (unknown author).

Physical:
- *Water—Drink 16–32 ounces at the following intervals:*
  - As soon as you wake up, before and after your meals, and before and after your workouts
- Meals—3 per day (meal prep is an excellent way to ensure success)
  - Weight loss option—35% protein, 40% fruits and vegetables, and 25% fat
  - Toning Option—40% protein, 35% fruits and vegetables, and 25% fats

- *Snacks—Refer to the approved optimal results list.*
    - Eat at least 4–5 snacks 1–2 hours before and/or after each meal.
- Workout—It's all about activity.
    - Wake-up plank—1 minute (please remember to stop your timer when you rest)
        - Side plank (switch sides at 30 seconds)
    - Strength exercises—1 minute each (please do 3–4 rounds)
        - Rest those muscles today
    - A 30-minute activity—change-it-up day
        - Go for a 30-minute bike ride, swim, or run.
        - Horseplay with a loved one for 30 minutes.
        - Go to an organized class, but don't overexert yourself.

Emotional:
Please do not forget to journal your experience.

_____

_____

_____

I love you all, and I will see you on the other side of the 21-day experience.

Coach K
#changeitupday #ismile

Hello, You Renewed team members! Congratulations on making it through day 4 and making it to day 5. Below is day 5.

Scripture:
Deuteronomy 31:6—"Be strong and courageous. Do not fear or be in dread of them, for it is the LORD your God who goes with you. He will not leave you or forsake you."

Goal:
Say this out loud: *I will see success (write your goal here)*

_____
_____
_____
_____
_____
_____

on the other side of my You Renewed 21-Day Experience!

Motivation:
"Life begins at the end of your comfort zone" (Unknown).

Physical:
- *Most important—Water. Drink 16–32 ounces at the following intervals:*
  - As soon as you wake up, before and after your meals, and before and after your workouts
- Meals—3 per day (meal prep is an excellent way to ensure success)
  - Weight loss option—35% protein, 40% fruits and vegetables, and 25% fat
  - Toning option—40% protein, 35% fruits and vegetables, and 25% fats
- *Snacks—Refer to the approved optimal results list.*
  - Eat at least 4–5 snacks 1–2 hours before and/or after each meal.

- Workout—a full-body day
  - Morning plank
    - Inchworm—Starting in the plank position, walk your hands back toward your feet, keeping your feet flat, and then back down in the plank position for 1 minute.
  - Strength exercises—1 minute each (please do 3–4 Rounds)
    - Inverted flyers
    - Mountain climbers
    - Bear crawl
  - 30-minute walk

Emotional:
Please do not forget to journal your experience.

_____

_____

_____

I love you all, and I will see you on the other side of the 21-day experience.

Coach K
#cardioday #ismile

YOU RENEWED

_____
_____
_____
_____
_____
_____
_____
_____
_____
_____
_____
_____
_____
_____
_____
_____
_____
_____
_____
_____
_____
_____
_____
_____
_____

Hello, You Renewed team members! Congratulations on making it through day 5 and making it to day 6. Below is day 6.

Scripture:
2 Samuel 23:12—"But he took his stand in the midst of the plot and defended it and struck down the Philistines, and the LORD worked a great victory."

Goal:
<u>Say this out loud:</u> *I will see success (write your goal here)*

_____
_____
_____
_____
_____
_____

on the other side of my You Renewed 21-Day Experience!

Motivation:
"You want me to do something...tell me I can't do it" (Maya Angelou).

Physical:
- *Most important—Water. Drink 16–32 ounces at the following intervals:*
  - As soon as you wake up, before and after your meals, and before and after your workouts
- Meals—3 per day (meal prep is an excellent way to ensure success)
  - Weight loss option—35% protein, 40% fruits and vegetables, and 25% fat
  - Toning option—40% protein, 35% fruits and vegetables, and 25% fats
- *Snacks—Refer to the approved optimal results list.*
  - Eat at least 4–5 snacks 1–2 hours before and/or after each meal.

- Workout—a full-body day
  - Morning plank
    - Regular plank
  - Strength exercises
    - Push-up single leg raise
    - Sprinter pulls
    - 1-2-3 hold
  - 30-minute walk

Emotional:
Please do not forget to journal your experience.

_____

_____

_____

I love you all, and I will see you on the other side of the 21-day experience.

Coach K
#fullbody #ismile

Hello, You Renewed team members! Congratulations on making it through day 6 and making it to day 7. *Reward yourself.* It's treat day. Below is day 7.

Scripture:
Genesis 2:3—"Then God blessed the seventh day and sanctified it, because in it He rested from all His work which God had created and made."

Goal:
<u>Say this out loud:</u> *I will see success (write your goal here)*
_____
_____
_____
_____
_____
_____

on the other side of my You Renewed 21-Day Experience!

Motivation:
"There are only 7 days in the week and 'someday' is not one of them" (Rita Chand).

Physical:
- *Most important—Water. Drink 16–32 ounces at the following intervals:*
  - As soon as you wake up, before and after your meals, and before and after your workouts
- Meals—3 per day (meal prep is an excellent way to ensure success)
  - Weight loss option—35% protein, 40% fruits and vegetables, and 25% fat
  - Toning option—40% protein, 35% fruits and vegetables, and 25% fats

- Snacks—It's a You Renewed treat day. Yes, a *treat*!
  - Ice cream, cake, chocolate, a treat
  - Don't get crazy! Only replace *one* of your snacks with a treat!
- Workout—It's a rest day.
  - Morning plank
    - How long can you hold your plank?
  - Strength exercises
    - It's a rest day
  - 30-minute walk

Emotional:
Please do not forget to journal your experience.

_____

_____

_____

I love you all, and I will see you on the other side of the 21-day experience.

Coach K
#treatday #ismile

_____
_____
_____
_____
_____
_____
_____
_____
_____
_____
_____
_____
_____
_____
_____
_____
_____
_____
_____
_____
_____
_____
_____

Hello, You Renewed team members! Congratulations on making it through week 1. Below is day 1 of week 2.

Scripture:
Psalm 37:23–24—"The steps of a man are established by the LORD, when he delights in his way though he fall, he shall not be cast headlong, for the LORD upholds his hand."

Goal:
Say this out loud: *I will see success (write your goal here)*

_____

_____

_____

_____

_____

on the other side of my You Renewed 21-Day Experience!

Motivation:
"You miss 100% of the shots you don't take" (Wayne Gretzky).

Physical:

- *Most important—Water. Drink 16–32 ounces at the following intervals:*
  - As soon as you wake up, before and after your meals, and before and after your workouts
- Meals—3 per day (meal prep is an excellent way to ensure success)
  - Weight loss option—35% protein, 40% fruits and vegetables, and 25% fat
  - Toning option—40% protein, 35% fruits and vegetables, and 25% fats
- *Snacks—Refer to the approved list for optimal results list.*
  - Eat at least 4–5 snacks 1–2 hours before and/or after each meal.

- Workout—a full-body day
  - Morning plank
    - Arm punches while in the plank position, alternate lifting each arm while punching the air in front of you.
  - Strength exercises—Please do 3–4 rounds of these challenging yoga poses.
    - 30-second downward facing dog
    - 30-second chaturanga hold
    - 30-second upward facing dog
  - 30-minute walk

Emotional:
Please do not forget to journal your experience.

_____

_____

_____

I love you all, and I will see you on the other side of the 21-day experience.

Coach K
#armday #ismile

Hello, You Renewed team members! Congratulations on making it through week 2 day 1! Below is day 2 of week 2.

Scripture:
Isaiah 40:31—"But they who wait for the LORD shall renew their strength; they shall mount up with wings like eagles; they shall run and not be weary; they shall walk and not faint."

Goal:
<u>Say this out loud: *I will see success (write your goal here)*</u>

_____

_____

_____

_____

_____

_____

on the other side of my You Renewed 21-Day Experience!

Motivation:
"You live longer once you realize that any time spent being unhappy is wasted" (Ruth E. Renkel).

Physical:
- *Most important—Water. Drink 16–32 ounces at the following intervals:*
  - As soon as you wake up, before and after your meals, and before and after your workouts
- Meals—3 per day (meal prep is an excellent way to ensure success)
  - Weight loss option—35% protein, 40% fruits and vegetables, and 25% fat
  - Toning option—40% protein, 35% fruits and vegetables, and 25% fats
- *Snacks—Refer to the approved optimal results list.*
  - Eat at least 4–5 snacks 1–2 hours before and/or after each meal.

- Workout—a leg day
  - Morning plank
    - Leg outs—While in the plank position, alternate stepping each leg to the side and back in.
  - Strength exercises
    - Yoga—warrior one
    - Yoga—warrior two
    - Yoga—warrior three
  - 30-minute walk

Emotional:
Please do not forget to journal your experience.

_____

_____

_____

I love you all, and I will see you on the other side of the 21-day experience.

Coach K
#legday #ismile

Hello, You Renewed team members! Congratulations on making it through week 2 day 2! Below is day 3 of week 2.

Scripture:
Psalm 37:5—"Commit your way to the LORD; trust in him, and he will act."

Goal:
Say this out loud: *I will see success (write your goal here)*

_____

_____

_____

_____

_____

on the other side of my You Renewed 21-Day Experience!

Motivation:
"Strength does not come from physical capacity. It comes from an indomitable will" (Mahatma Gandhi).

Physical:
- *Most important—Water. Drink 16–32 ounces at the following intervals:*
  - As soon as you wake up, before and after your meals, and before and after your workouts
- Meals—3 per day (meal prep is an excellent way to ensure success)
  - Weight loss option—35% protein, 40% fruits and vegetables, and 25% fat
  - Toning option—40% protein, 35% fruits and vegetables, and 25% fats
- *Snacks—Refer to the approved optimal results list.*
  - Eat at least 4–5 snacks 1–2 hours before and/or after each meal.

- Workout—an ab day
  - Morning plank
    - Hip squeezes—While in the plank position, rotate your hips side to side trying to reach the floor.
  - Strength exercises
    - Boat pose
    - Spine spiral
    - Down dog crunch
  - 30-minute walk

Emotional:
Please do not forget to journal your experience.

_____

_____

_____

I love you all, and I will see you on the other side of the 21-day experience.

Coach K
#absday #ismile

Hello, You Renewed team members! Congratulations on making it through week 2 day 3! Below is day 4 of week 2. You made it over the *hump*! Woo-hoo! It's results day!

Scripture:
Matthew 19:26—"But Jesus looked at them and said, 'With man this is impossible, but with God all things are possible.'"

Goal:
Say this out loud: *I will see success (write your goal here)*
_____
_____
_____

on the other side of my You Renewed 21-Day Experience!

Motivation:
"Motivation will almost always beat mere talent" (Norman R. Augustine).

Physical:
- *Most important—Water. Drink 16–32 ounces at the following intervals:*
  - As soon as you wake up, before and after your meals, and before and after your workouts
- Meals—3 per day (meal prep is an excellent way to ensure success)
  - Weight loss option—35% protein, 40% fruits and vegetables, and 25% fat
  - Toning option—40% protein, 35% fruits and vegetables, and 25% fats
- *Snacks—Refer to the approved optimal results list.*
  - Eat at least 4–5 snacks 1–2 hours before and/or after each meal.

- Workout—It's results day.
  - Morning plank
    - Plank hold (How long can you hold your plank? It was longer than last time, wasn't it? *Woo-hoo!*)
  - Strength exercises
    - Rest
  - A fun activity
    - Horseplay with a loved one.
    - Go for a bike ride.
    - Play an interactive video game with a mentee, sibling, child, or friend.

Emotional:
Please do not forget to journal your experience.

_____

_____

_____

I love you all, and I will see you on the other side of the 21-day experience.

Coach K
#resultsday #changeitup #ismile

Hello, You Renewed team members! Congratulations on making it through week 2 day 5! Below is day 5 of week 2.

Scripture:
Mark 9:23—"And Jesus said to him, 'If you can!' All things are possible for one who believes."

Motivation:
"Motivation will almost always beat mere talent" (Norman R. Augustine).

Goal:
Say this out loud: *I will see success (write your goal here)*

_____

_____

_____

_____

_____

on the other side of my You Renewed 21-Day Experience!

Physical:
- *Most important—Water. Drink 16–32 ounces at the following intervals:*
  - As soon as you wake up, before and after your meals, and before and after your workouts
- Meals—3 per day (meal prep is an excellent way to ensure success)
  - Weight loss option—35% protein, 40% fruits and vegetables, and 25% fat
  - Toning option—40 protein, 35% fruits and vegetables, and 25% fats
- *Snacks*—Eat at least 4–5 snacks 1–2 hours before and/or after each meal.

- Workout—full-body day
    - Morning plank
        - Plank knee twists—While in the plank position, rotate.
    - Strength exercises
        - Tree pose
        - Superman
        - Bridge
    - 30-minute walk

Emotional:
Please do not forget to journal your experience.

_____

_____

I love you all, and I will see you on the other side of the 21-day experience.

Coach K
#fullbody #ismile

Hello, You Renewed team members! Congratulations on making it through week 2 day 5! Below is day 6 of week 2.

Scripture:
Philippians 4:13—"I can do all things through him who strengthens me" (from the Apostle Paul).

Motivation:
"Nothing great was ever achieved without enthusiasm" (Ralph Waldo Emerson).

Goal:
Say this out loud: *I will see success (write your goal here)*

_____

_____

_____

_____

_____

on the other side of my You Renewed 21-Day Experience!

Physical:
- *Most important*—Water. Drink 16–32 ounces at the following intervals:
  - As soon as you wake up, before and after your meals, and before and after your workouts
- Meals—3 per day (meal prep is an excellent way to ensure success)
  - Weight loss option—35% protein, 40% fruits and vegetables, and 25% fat
  - Toning option—40% protein, 35% fruits and vegetables, and 25% fats
- *Snacks*—Eat at least 4–5 snacks 1–2 hours before and/or after each meal.

- Workout—It's a cardio day (let's get that heart rate up).
  - Morning plank
    - Plank jumps
  - Strength exercises
    - 30-second jumping jacks—30-second push-up to child's pose
    - 30-second squat heal tap—30-second leg lift pigeon
    - 30-second lateral jumps—30-second warrior lunge
  - 30-minute walk

Emotional:
Please do not forget to journal your experience.

_____
_____
_____

I love you all, and I will see you on the other side of the 21-day experience.

Coach K
#cardioday #ismile

_____
_____
_____
_____
_____
_____
_____
_____
_____
_____
_____
_____
_____
_____
_____
_____
_____
_____
_____
_____
_____
_____
_____

Hello, You Renewed team members! Congratulations on making it through week 2 day 6 and making it to week 2 day 7. Below is day 7. It's a You Renewed treat day!

Scripture:
Genesis 2:3—"So God blessed the seventh day and made it holy, because on it God rested from all his work that he had done in creation."

Goal:
Say this out loud: *I will see success (write your goal here)*

_____

_____

_____

_____

_____

_____

on the other side of my You Renewed 21-Day Experience!

Motivation:
Wake up with determination. Go to be with satisfaction.

Physical:
- *Most important—Water. Drink 16–32 ounces at the following intervals:*
  - As soon as you wake up, before and after your meals, and before and after your workouts
- Meals—3 per day (meal prep is an excellent way to ensure success)
  - Weight loss option—35% protein, 40% fruits and vegetables, and 25% fat
  - Toning option—40% protein, 35% fruits and vegetables, and 25% fats

- Treat day—It's a You Renewed treat day. Yes, a treat!
  - Ice cream, cake, chocolate, a treat
  - Don't get crazy! Only replace *one* of your snacks with a treat!
- *Snacks—Refer to the approved optimal results list.*
  - Eat at least 4–5 snacks 1–2 hours before and/or after dinner.
- Workout—It's a rest day.
  - Morning plank
    - How long can you hold your plank?—This is *optional.*
  - Strength exercises
    - It's a rest day.
  - 30-minute walk

Emotional:
Please do not forget to journal your experience.

_____

_____

_____

I love you all, and I will see you on the other side of the 21-day experience.

Coach K
#treatday #ismile

Hello, You Renewed team members! Congratulations and welcome to week 3 day 1.

Scripture:
Ephesians 6:13—"Therefore take up the whole armor of God, that you may be able to withstand in the evil day, and having done all, to stand firm."

Goal:
<u>Say this out loud: *I will see success (write your goal here)*</u>

_____

_____

_____

_____

_____

_____

on the other side of my You Renewed 21-Day Experience!

Motivation:
"Insanity: doing the same thing over and over again and expecting different results" (Albert Einstein).

Physical:
- *Most important—Water. Drink 16–32 ounces at the following intervals:*
  - As soon as you wake up, before and after your meals, and before and after your workouts
- Meals—3 per day (meal prep is an excellent way to ensure success)
  - Weight loss option—35% protein, 40% fruits and vegetables, and 25% fat
  - Toning option—40% protein, 35% fruits and vegetables, and 25% fats
- *Snacks—Refer to the approved optimal results list.*
  - Eat at least 4–5 snacks 1–2 hours before and/or after dinner.

- Workout—It's arm day.
  - Morning plank
    - Plank in and outs
  - Strength exercises—Challenge yourself and add weights but no more than 10% of your body weight.
    - Full-length hammer curl
    - Biceps curls ups
    - Triceps kickbacks
  - 30-minute walk

Emotional:
Please do not forget to journal your experience.

_____
_____
_____

_____

I love you all, and I will see you on the other side of the 21-day experience.

Coach K
#armday #ismile

Hello, You Renewed team members! Congratulations and welcome to day 2 of week 3.

Scripture:
Colossians 3:23–24—"Whatever you do, work heartily, as for the Lord and not for men, knowing that from the Lord you will receive the inheritance as your reward. You are serving the Lord Christ."

Goal:
Say this out loud: *I will see success (write your goal here)*

_____

_____

_____

_____

_____

_____

on the other side of my You Renewed 21-Day Experience!

Motivation:
"Ability is what you're capable of doing. Motivation determines what you do. Attitude determines how well you do it" (Lou Holtz).

Physical:
- *Most important—Water. Drink 16–32 ounces at the following intervals:*
  - As soon as you wake up, before and after your meals, and before and after your workouts
- Meals—3 per day (meal prep is an excellent way to ensure success)
  - Weight loss option—35% protein, 40% fruits and vegetables, and 25% fat
  - Toning option—40% protein, 35% fruits and vegetables, and 25% fats
- *Snacks—Refer to the approved optimal results list.*
  - Eat at least 4–5 snacks 1–2 hours before and/or after each meal.

- Workout—It's leg day.
  - Morning plank
    - Plank dirty dog
  - Strength exercises—Want to challenge yourself, add weights but no more than 10% of your body weight.
    - Front squats
    - Side lunge
    - Gluteus lunge
  - 30-minute walk

Emotional:
Please do not forget to journal your experience.

_____

_____

_____

I love you all, and I will see you on the other side of the 21-day experience.

Coach K
#legday #ismile

Hello, You Renewed team members! Congratulations and welcome to day 3 of week 3, day 17!

Scripture:
1 Timothy 4:12—"Don't let anyone put you down because you're young. Teach believers with your life: by word, by demeanor, by love, by faith, by integrity."

Goal:
<u>Say this out Loud:</u> *I will see success (write your goal here)*
_____
_____
_____
_____
_____
_____

on the other side of my You Renewed 21-Day Experience!

Motivation:
"Motivation is what gets you started. Habit is what keeps you going" (Jim Ryan).

Physical:
- *Most important—Water. Drink 16–32 ounces at the following intervals:*
    - As soon as you wake up, before and after your meals, and before and after your workouts
- Meals—3 per day (meal prep is an excellent way to ensure success)
    - Weight loss option—35% protein, 40% fruits and vegetables, and 25% fat
    - Toning option—40% protein, 35% fruits and vegetables, and 25% fats
- *Snacks—Refer to the approved optimal results list.*
    - Eat at least 4–5 snacks 1–2 hours before and/or after each meal.

- Workout—It's core day.
  - Morning plank
    - Bird dog plank
  - Strength exercises—Want to challenge yourself, add weights but no more than 10% of your body weight.
    - Reverse crunch
    - Russian twist
    - Wood chop
  - 30-minute walk

Emotional:
Please do not forget to journal your experience.

_____

_____

_____

I love you all, and I will see you on the other side of the 21-day experience.

Coach K
#absday #ismile

YOU RENEWED

Hello, You Renewed team members! Congratulations and welcome to day 4 of week 3, day 18! Results day!

Scripture:
1 Timothy 4:8—"For while bodily training is of some value, godliness is of value in every way, as it holds promise for the present life and also for the life to come."

Goal:
Say this out loud: *I will see success (write your goal here)*

_____

_____

_____

_____

_____

on the other side of my You Renewed 21-Day Experience!

Motivation:
"I've missed more than 9,000 shots in my career. I've lost almost 300 games. 26 times, I've been trusted to take the game winning shot and missed. I've failed over and over and over again in my life. And that is why I succeed" (Michael Jordan).

Physical:

- *Most important—Water. Drink 16–32 ounces at the following intervals:*
  - As you wake up, before and after your meals, and before and after your workouts
- Meals—3 per day (meal prep is an excellent way to ensure success)
  - Weight loss option—35% protein, 40% fruits and vegetables, and 25% fat
  - Toning option—40% protein, 35% fruits and vegetables, and 25% fats

- *Snacks—Refer to the approved optimal results list.*
  - Eat at least 4–5 snacks 1–2 hours before and/or after each meal.
- Workout—It's results day.
  - Morning plank
    - How long can you hold your morning plank?
  - Strength exercises
    - Rest those muscles.
  - 30-minute walk
    - Horseplay with a loved one.
    - Play an interactive video game with a mentee, sibling, child, or friend.

Emotional:
Please do not forget to journal your experience.

_____

_____

I love you all, and I will see you on the other side of the 21-day experience.

Coach K
#resultsday #changeitup #ismile

Hello, You Renewed team members! Congratulations and welcome to day 5 of week 3, day 19!

Scripture:
Hebrews 12:11—"For the moment all discipline seems painful rather than pleasant, but later it yields the peaceful fruit of righteousness to those who have been trained by it."

Goal:
Say this out loud: *I will see success (write your goal here)*

_____

_____

_____

_____

_____

on the other side of my You Renewed 21-Day Experience!

Motivation:
"Fear is what stops you...courage is what keeps you going" (Unknown).

Physical:
- *Most important—Water. Drink 16–32 ounces at the following intervals:*
  - As soon as you wake up, before and after your meals, and before and after your workouts
- Meals—3 per day (meal prep is an excellent way to ensure success)
  - Weight loss option—35% protein, 40% fruits and vegetables, and 25% fat
  - Toning option—40% protein, 35% fruits and vegetables, and 25% fats
- *Snacks—Refer to the approved optimal results list.*
  - Eat at least 4–5 snacks 1–2 hours before and/or after each meal.

- Workout—It's a full-body day
  - Morning plank
    - *T* plank
  - Strength exercises
    - Mountain steppers
    - Single leg raise push-up
    - Lunge with elbow instep
  - 30-minute walk

Emotional:
Please do not forget to journal your experience.

_____
_____
_____

I love you all, and I will see you on the other side of the 21-day experience.

Coach K
#fullbodyday #ismile

YOU RENEWED

_____
_____
_____
_____
_____
_____
_____
_____
_____
_____
_____
_____
_____
_____
_____
_____
_____
_____
_____
_____
_____
_____

Hello, You Renewed team members! Congratulations and welcome to day 6 of week 3, day 20!

Scripture:
Hebrews 12:12–13—"Therefore lift your drooping hands and strengthen your weak knees, and make straight paths for your feet, so that what is lame may not be put out of joint but rather be healed."

Motivation:
"In seeking happiness for others, you find it for yourself" (Anonymous).

Goal:
Say this out loud: *I will see success (write your goal here)*

_____

_____

_____

_____

_____

on the other side of my You Renewed 21-Day Experience!

Physical:
- Most important—Water. Drink 16–32 ounces at the following intervals:
  - As soon as you wake up, before and after your meals, and before and after your workouts
- Meals—3 per day (meal prep is an excellent way to ensure success)
  - Weight loss option—35% protein, 40% fruits and vegetables, and 25% fat
  - Toning option—40% protein, 35% fruits and vegetables, and 25% fats
- *Snacks*—Eat at least 4–5 snacks 1–2 hours before and/or after each meal.

- Workout—It's a cardio day (let's get that heart rate up).
  - Morning plank
    - Plank bursts
  - Strength exercises
    - Burpees
    - Ladder climbers
    - 1-2-3 holds
  - 30-minute walk

Emotional:
Please do not forget to journal your experience.

_____

_____

_____

I love you all, and I will see you on the other side of the 21-day experience.

Coach K
#cardioday #ismile

Hello, You Renewed team members! Congratulations, *you made it to day 21. Reward yourself.* It's treat day!

Scripture:
Philippians 2:1–2—"If you've gotten anything at all out of following Christ, if his love has made any difference in your life, if being in a community of the Spirit means anything to you, if you have a heart, if you care—then do me a favor: Agree with each other, love each other, be deep-spirited friends."

Goal:
Say this out loud: *I will see success (write your goal here)*

_____

_____

_____

_____

_____

on the other side of my You Renewed 21-Day Experience!

Motivation:
"The finish line is just the beginning of a whole new race" (unknown).

Physical:
- *Most important—Water. Drink 16–32 ounces at the following intervals:*
    - As soon as you wake up, before and after your meals, and before and after your workouts
- Meals—3 per day (meal prep is an excellent way to ensure success)
    - Weight loss option—35% protein, 40% fruits and vegetables, and 25% fat
    - Toning option—40% protein, 35% fruits and vegetables, and 25% fats

- Snacks—It's a You Renewed treat day. Yes a *treat*!
  - Ice cream, cake, chocolate, a treat
  - Don't get crazy! Only replace *one* of your snacks with a treat!
- Workout—It's a rest day.
  - Morning plank
    - How long can you hold your plank? How did you do?
  - Strength exercises
    - Rest those muscles. *You deserve it!*
  - 30-minute walk—*Celebrate your achievement.*

Emotional:
Please do not forget to journal your experience.

_____

_____

_____

I love you all, and I will see you on the other side of the 21-day experience.

Coach K
#YouRenewed21 #ismile

Congratulations, You Renewed team members! *You made it!* The program is 21 days; however, whether you are on day 4, day 15, or day 21, I am so very proud of you because you have made it to the other side of *your* You Renewed experience.

Remember, this program is yours. You can pick it up anytime, and start from any point. As long as you follow the process of the day or days you are selecting, you will see success with **You Renewed** goal.

Again, congratulations on making it to the other side of your experience, and I look forward to seeing you here again and again and again.

Sincerely,
Coach K

PS: If you have any questions, comments, or suggestions, please email Coach K at YouRenewedExperience@gmail.com.

Your You Renewed
Experience Appendix

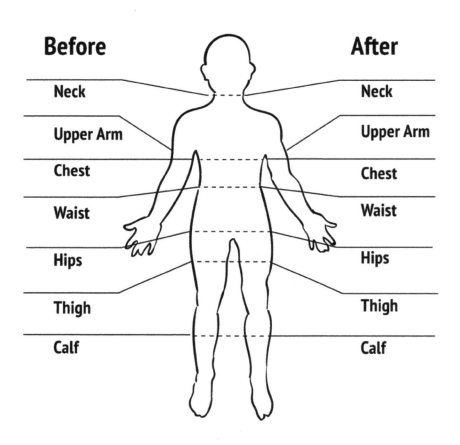

Before

Neck

Upper Arm

Chest

Waist

Hips

Thigh

Calf

After

Neck

Upper Arm

Chest

Waist

Hips

Thigh

Calf

Your You Renewed Experience
Foods to Eat and
Example Meal Plans

You Renewed Foods to Eat and Avoid

Foods to Avoid	Foods to Enjoy			
	Meat	Fruits	Vegetables	Fats
White flour and all products using it: • Hominy and pasta • Fried foods • Carbonated beverages including diet sodas • Foods containing preservatives or additives • Refined sugar • High-fructose corn syrup • Chemical sugar substitutes • Margarine shortening	All meat	Apples Apricots Avocados Bananas Berries Blackberries Blueberries Boysenberries Breadfruit Cantaloupe Cherries Coconuts Cranberries Dates and figs Grapefruit Grapes Grenadine Guava Honeydew Melons Kiwi Lemons Limes Mangoes Melons Mulberry Nectarines Oats and olives Oranges Papayas Peaches Pears Pineapples Plums and prunes Raisins Raspberries Strawberries Tangelos Tangerines Watermelon	Tip: When cooking vegetables, steam or roast them. Do not overcook them. Artichokes Asparagus beets Broccoli Brussels sprouts Cabbage and carrots Cauliflower and celery Chili peppers Corn and cucumbers Eggplant, garlic, gingerroot, kale, leeks, lettuce, mushrooms, mustard, greens okra, onions, parsley, any peppers, any potatoes, radishes, rutabagas, scallions, spinach sprouts, squashes, sweet potatoes, tomatoes, turnips, watercress, yams zucchini, jasmine rice, oatmeal of wheat, and Ezekiel bread	Cheese butter Sour cream Plain yogurt Brazil nuts Almonds Macadamia nuts Pecans Walnuts Pine nuts Avocado Coconut oil Avocado oil Pork grinds

You Renewed Experience Approved Snack List

Any fruit	A small wedge of	1 egg anyway you	3 sweet pickles—*no*
Any fresh vegetable	Brie	want it	*sugar added*
3 ounces of deli turkey	3 hearty stalks of	Figs, fresh (3) or	2 fresh pineapple
Spread with Dijon	broccoli	dried (2)	slices
Mustard and rolled in	1 1/2 cups cooked	Fish: A slice of	4 fresh plums
Romaine or Boston	brussels sprouts	flounder, halibut, and	1 medium baked
Lettuce leaves	1 medium baked	haddock,	potato with butter *or*
5 fresh apricots	potatoes cooked	1 bratwurst	sour cream (do not
1 large artichoke	3 cups of fresh	1 hotdog	combine both)
30 spears of steamed	cabbage	1 cup fresh fruit salad	4 dried prunes
Fresh asparagus	1 wedge cheese	1/2 cup gefilte fish	(another sweetener)
1/4 avocado	1/2 cantaloupe	1 grapefruit	A small handful of
1/2 cup of edamame	2 cups of fresh or	A large bunch of	raisins
3/4 cup mango tossed	steamed carrots	grapes (40)	1 glass of red wine
with lime juice	3 cups of fresh or	1 slice of ham	5 sardines
Red pepper flakes	steamed cauliflower	1 very small	15 shrimp
2 slices of broiled	6 cups of celery	hamburger patty	2 cups cooked
bacon	1 inch cube of	3/4 honeydew melon	spinach
1 large banana	cheddar	1 1/2 cups kale	3 cups of squash,
3/4 cup lima beans,	1 cup of cherries	2 heads lettuce	boiled
cooked	(excellent for getting	Make a dressing by	2 cups of fresh
(Tip for beans, to cut	rid of inflammation)	putting avocado	strawberries
the effects of gas,	A slice of broiled or	onions and tomatoes	1/2 sweet potatoes
cook the beans,	roasted chicken	in the blender with	Tangerines (2)
then rinse the beans	6 clams	apple cider vinegar	Tomatoes (3)
with cool water, and then	A small cappuccino	and olive oil.	1/4 cup tuna fish
warm them again.)	with half-and-half	2/3 cups lobster	1 slice of turkey
4 cups of green beans	1/2 cup fresh	1 slice of any	1 cup vegetable soup
1 slice of corned beef	crabmeat	luncheon meat	10 walnut halves
1 cup jicama sticks	2 tbsp. cream cheese	10 fresh mushrooms	4 bunches of
with 2 tablespoons of	spread on celery	8 mussels	watercress
hummus for dipping	sticks	25 pieces of okra	1 glass of white wine

1 slice of lean loin of beef 1 lean rib of beef 1 beer 4 cooked, fresh beets, 40 blackberries, 1 cup of blueberries, 1 3 oz piece of bluefish, baked or broiled	2 tablespoons of cream cheese with onion powder and pepper and unlimited celery sticks large cucumbers dates (an excellent sweetener as well) 2 dates with natural peanut or almond butter	16 extra-large olives 2/3 of a bowl of onion soup A big orange 2 peaches 20 peanuts roasted 1 pear 3/4 cups of green peas Green peppers Dill pickles	If you just have to have some kind of Grain, eat tortillas made with corn or flax seed

Example 7-Day You Renewed Meal Plan

Monday	Tuesday	Wednesday	Thursday	Friday	Saturday	Sunday
Wake up: 16–32 ounces of water						
Breakfast: Smoothie I eat a smoothie for breakfast every morning. 1/2 cup frozen blueberries 1/2 cup frozen cherries (great for inflammation) 1/2 cup frozen spinach 1 cup aloe vera juice (you can use almond milk or coconut milk as well) 1 tbsp. coconut oil 1 tsp. cinnamon (great for inflammation) 1 tsp. turmeric (great for inflammation) 1 tsp. powdered vitamin C 1 tbsp. psyllium husk						*Breakfast: One serving of each* Turkey, cheese, tomato or salsa spinach, omelet, and avocado
Approved snack						
Lunch Salmon, broiled broccoli, and hummus	*Lunch* Cucumber tomato salad, grapes, green beans, and avocado	*Lunch* Green beans, broccoli, cucumber salad, cheese sticks, and hummus	*Lunch* Teriyaki chicken, one egg, and grapes	*Lunch* Spinach, chickpeas, tomatoes, cucumber, olives, and cheese salad	Lunch Tuna, hard-boiled egg, pickles, and mus-tard salad, hummus, and mixed vegetables	Lunch Chicken, spinach, mushroom, tomatoes, and chickpea salad
Approved Snack						
Dinner Grilled garlic chicken, green beans, grapes, and black-eyed peas	*Dinner* Taco Tuesday Huevos Con Rancheros, black beans, corn tortillas, and salsa	*Dinner* Baked french fries, cucum-ber tomato salad, and zucchini bun cheese burger	*Dinner* Bratwurst, fruit salad, green beans, and Ezekiel toast	*Dinner* Hibachi chicken, mush-rooms, baby corn, and grapes	Dinner Do some research on how to make vegetarian coconut tom yum soup	Dinner Roast, carrots, red pota-toes, grapes, and baked apples with cinnamon
Approved snack						
Herbal tea. *Don't forget about your water intake.*						

You Renewed Example Recipes

Breakfast: Taco Tuesday Omelet	Dessert: Lemon-Glazed Pound Cake
Ingredients 1/2 lb. red potatoes peeled and diced or shredded 2 tbsp. extra virgin olive oil, avocado oil, or coconut oil 1/4 c. diced red onion 1 clove garlic, minced 2 large whole eggs, lightly whipped 1 egg white, lightly whipped 1 tsp. of parsley 1 tsp. of oregano 1 tsp. of paprika Pink or sea salt and pepper to taste Makes 2 servings (1 omelet per serving). Directions • In a large pan, add potatoes. Cover with water, and bring to boil. Cook uncovered for 3 minutes. Remove from heat. Cover and let stand for about 10 minutes or until potatoes are tender, not mushy. Drain well. • In a deep 10-inch nonstick skillet, heat oil over medium heat. Add onion and garlic. Cook for about 8 minutes, stirring occasionally. Add potatoes and cook an additional 5 minutes. • Combine whole eggs and egg whites. Stir in parsley, oregano, and paprika. Season with salt if desired. Pour mixture over potatoes in hot skillet. Reduce heat and cook uncovered for about 10 minutes or until bottom of omelet is golden. • If desired, brown top under toaster oven. Garnish with fresh herb sprigs, salsa, or guacamole. Serve immediately.	Pound Cake Wet Ingredients 8 large eggs at room temperature 8 oz. of room temperature cream cheese 1/2 c. of room temperature unsalted butter 2 tsp. of vanilla extract 1/2 c. of full-fat sour cream Dry Ingredients 1 1/2 c. coconut flour 4 tsp. of baking powder 1 1/2 c. granulated sugar substitute 1/2 tsp. of sea salt or 1/4 tsp. pink salt Lemon Glaze Ingredients 1 c. of confectioners' sugar substitute 2 tbsp. of lemon juice 1/2 tsp. of lemon extract 1 tbsp. of grated lemon rind Directions - Preheat oven to 350 degrees. - Generously grease 10-inch (preferably nonstick) pan with butter. - In your favorite medium-sized mixing bowl, combine your coconut flour, baking powder, and sea/pink salt. Set aside. - In your favorite large-sized mixing bowl using a handheld electric or stand-up mixer, beat together the butter, cream cheese, sugar substitute, and vanilla extract until light and fluffy.

	- Add the 8 eggs one at a time to the butter and cream cheese mixture, scraping the bowl regularly. Note: Due to the large number of eggs, the wet mixture will *not* fully combine until the dry ingredients are added. - Slowly add the dry ingredients to the wet ingredients, allowing mix speed setting, scraping the bowl regularly. - Note: The batter will be *very* thick and fluffy. This is due to the use of coconut flour. - Spread the thick and fluffy batter into the generously greased loaf pan. - Bake the cake for 1 1/4–1 1/2 hours (75–90 minutes). At the 1-hour baking point, check the cake with a toothpick. If the toothpick comes out clean with just a tiny amount of cake crumb, it is completely baked/done. If not done, allow the cake to bake for the necessary additional time. (Go to step 11 to make the lemon glaze.) - Allow your cooked cake to cool in the pan for about 10 minutes. Unmold the cake, and allow to cool on a baking rack for 20 minutes. (Go to step 12.) - While the cake is baking, combine all the ingredients in the icing except the grated lemon peel. (Go to step 10.) - Once the cake is fully cooled, add the icing by drizzling it to the top of the cake, allowing it to drizzle down the sides. Sprinkle the top of the glaze with the grated lemon peel.

About the Author

Kenisha Bell, otherwise known as Coach K, is a title-holding professional natural figure bodybuilding competitor and writer of *You Renewed 21-Day Experience*. She is a single mother of a young son, the other half of the dynamic Team Ken&Ken, a respected personal trainer in her church community, and a lean six-sigma continuous improvement professional. Coach K does her best work when you allow her to meet you where you are and take you where you want to go. Her passion for continuous improvement has transformed the mind, body, and souls of many and will for you and many to come.